BRITISH CASTLES

TOP **50** TO VISIT

BONDI PUBLISHING

INTRODUCTION

Castles have long captured the imagination, standing as timeless symbols of power, history, and mystery. From towering fortifications designed to ward off invaders to opulent residences of royalty, these magnificent structures tell stories of battles, political intrigue, and cultural evolution. The British Isles, with its rich and complex history, is home to some of the most awe-inspiring castles in the world. From the majestic cliffs of Scotland to the lush landscapes of Wales, and the rolling hills of England to the rugged coastline of Northern Ireland, each castle is a portal to a different era.

This book takes you on a journey to 50 of the best castles to visit in Britain—each one unique, brimming with fascinating history, and offering unparalleled beauty. Whether you're wandering through the ancient stone corridors of Windsor Castle or gazing out from the dramatic heights of Dunnottar Castle, you'll find yourself immersed in the stories of the monarchs, warriors, and everyday people who once walked these halls.

As you explore these majestic fortresses, you'll not only encounter the architectural marvels of medieval engineering but also the legends, dramas, and triumphs that shaped the course of British history. Whether you're an avid historian, an architecture enthusiast, or simply someone in search of a breathtaking view, this collection of castles will inspire awe and wonder as it brings the past to life, one stone at a time.

Join us on a journey through time and discover the fortresses that have defined Britain's past, protected its people, and captured the imaginations of generations.

The Bondi Publishing Team

CONTENTS

BONDI PUBLISHING

WINDSOR CASTLE
BERKSHIRE, ENGLAND

HISTORICAL SIGNIFICANCE

Windsor Castle is the oldest and largest inhabited castle in the world, dating back to the 11th century when it was founded by William the Conqueror. It has been the home of British kings and queens for over 1,000 years, serving as a royal residence and a fortress. Today, it remains the official residence of the British monarch and a place for ceremonial events. It has witnessed many significant moments in British history, including royal weddings, state banquets, and the changing of the guard.

LOCATION

Windsor Castle is located in Windsor, Berkshire, about 20 miles west of London, perched on a hill overlooking the River Thames. Its strategic location has made it an important royal stronghold for centuries.

ARCHITECTURAL FEATURES

The castle's design has evolved over the centuries, combining medieval, Georgian, and Victorian architecture. Key features include the Round Tower, the State Apartments, St George's Chapel (a fine example of Gothic architecture), and the Lower Ward. The castle is surrounded by a large park, and the walls are dotted with crenellations and battlements. The iconic Long Walk offers sweeping views of the surrounding countryside.

INTERESTING FACTS

- Windsor Castle is still used for royal ceremonies, including the annual St George's Day service and the State Opening of Parliament.
- Queen Elizabeth II spent much of her time at Windsor Castle during the COVID-19 pandemic, as it became a retreat for the royal family.
- The castle was heavily damaged by fire in 1992 but was restored with the help of donations from the public and the royal family.

NOTEWORTHY SURROUNDINGS

The castle is located within Windsor Great Park, which is perfect for scenic walks. The town of Windsor, with its quaint streets and traditional shops, is also worth exploring. Nearby is the famous Eton College, known for educating British royalty and political leaders. The River Thames runs through the town, offering boat trips and beautiful riverside views.

TOWER OF LONDON
LONDON, ENGLAND

HISTORICAL SIGNIFICANCE

The Tower of London has been at the heart of British history since its founding by William the Conqueror in 1066. Originally built as a royal fortress and palace, it later became notorious as a prison, execution site, and treasury. It housed the Crown Jewels and was the site of numerous royal executions, including those of Anne Boleyn and Thomas More. The Tower also served as the royal menagerie for exotic animals, such as lions and elephants. Today, it is a UNESCO World Heritage site.

LOCATION

The Tower of London is situated on the north bank of the River Thames, in central London, close to iconic landmarks such as Tower Bridge and the City of London.

ARCHITECTURAL FEATURES

The Tower complex includes several buildings, the most famous of which is the White Tower, which is the oldest part and a prime example of Norman military architecture. Other key structures include the Bloody Tower, the Tower Green (where executions took place), and the Medieval Palace. The castle's defensive walls are still intact, and the moat surrounding it has been drained.

INTERESTING FACTS

- The Tower of London is home to the Crown Jewels, including the British monarchy's regalia used in coronations.
- The ravens that live at the Tower are part of a legend: if they ever leave, it's said the kingdom will fall.
- The Tower was a royal residence, but it became notorious for its use as a prison, where many high-profile prisoners were held before execution.

NOTEWORTHY SURROUNDINGS

Located near the heart of London, the Tower is surrounded by the modern cityscape. Tower Bridge, which spans the River Thames, is a short walk away, offering stunning views of the Tower and the river. The area is also home to the historic St. Katharine Docks, a marina with restaurants and shops.

DOVER CASTLE
KENT, ENGLAND

Dover Castle, known as the "Key to England," has played a crucial role in England's defense for over 2,000 years. Its origins date back to Roman times, but the current structure largely dates from the 12th century. Dover Castle was vital during various conflicts, including the Napoleonic Wars and World War II. Its strategic location near the English Channel made it essential for the defense of England from invasions. The castle also served as a royal residence for several kings, including Henry II.

LOCATION

Dover Castle is located in Dover, Kent, on the southeastern coast of England. It offers commanding views of the English Channel, making it an ideal location for monitoring the sea approaches.

ARCHITECTURAL FEATURES

Dover Castle's architecture reflects its long history, with additions from the Romans, Normans, and medieval periods. The most iconic feature is the keep, a massive stone tower that was the center of the medieval fortress. The castle also has a complex of underground tunnels, used during World War II for military operations. The Roman lighthouse, still standing, is one of the oldest structures in Britain.

INTERESTING FACTS

- During World War II, Dover Castle served as a military command center, including for the Dunkirk evacuation.
- The tunnels beneath the castle were rediscovered in the 20th century and are now open to visitors.
- Dover Castle's positioning made it a key site for detecting enemy ships crossing the English Channel.

NOTEWORTHY SURROUNDINGS

The castle overlooks the town of Dover and the famous White Cliffs, which offer stunning views of the Channel. Nearby is the South Foreland Lighthouse, and the picturesque coastal walk along the cliffs provides scenic views. The town of Dover itself has a rich maritime history and a beautiful harbor.

ARUNDEL CASTLE
WEST SUSSEX, ENGLAND

Arundel Castle dates back to 1067, when it was built by Roger de Montgomery, a Norman nobleman. It has remained in the hands of the Howard family for centuries and is one of the best-preserved castles in England. The castle played an important role during the English Civil War and has been expanded and modified over the centuries. It remains the ancestral home of the Duke of Norfolk, the head of the Catholic aristocracy in England.

LOCATION

Arundel Castle is located in the small town of Arundel, West Sussex, in southern England. It sits on a hill overlooking the River Arun and the surrounding countryside.

ARCHITECTURAL FEATURES

The castle is an excellent example of Norman architecture, with a striking medieval keep and a large gatehouse. The interiors are a mix of medieval and Victorian styles, with grand state rooms and impressive collections of art and furniture. The castle's grounds include beautiful formal gardens, with a particularly famous rose garden.

INTERESTING FACTS

- The castle has been the residence of the Duke of Norfolk since the 17th century, and it remains a private family home.
- Arundel Castle played a role during the English Civil War, with the royalist forces holding the castle against the Parliamentarians.
- The castle's grounds include one of the largest private collections of armour in Britain.

NOTEWORTHY SURROUNDINGS

The castle's location in the picturesque town of Arundel offers beautiful views of the surrounding countryside. The town itself is known for its charming streets, antique shops, and the nearby Arundel Wetland Centre, a nature reserve with abundant wildlife. The South Downs National Park is nearby, providing opportunities for scenic walks and exploration.

DURHAM CASTLE
COUNTY DURHAM, ENGLAND

Durham Castle, a UNESCO World Heritage site, was originally built by the Normans in the 11th century to serve as a fortress and residence for the Prince Bishops of Durham. The castle's strategic location on a hill overlooking the River Wear was chosen to protect the region from potential invasions. Over the centuries, it has served as both a military stronghold and an episcopal residence. Today, Durham Castle is part of Durham University and is used as a college hall, but its historical roots remain deeply intertwined with the governance of northern England.

LOCATION

Durham Castle is located in the city of Durham, County Durham, in northeast England. The castle stands on a high hill, offering stunning views of the surrounding countryside and the medieval city of Durham, which is also known for its iconic cathedral.

ARCHITECTURAL FEATURES

The castle's architecture is a fascinating mix of medieval and later alterations. The Norman keep, which dates back to the 11th century, is the centerpiece of the castle, while the rest of the structure was expanded and altered over the centuries. The castle features vaulted ceilings, a chapel, and a large courtyard. Its fortified walls and towers remain prominent, while the interiors have been modified to suit the needs of a modern university.

INTERESTING FACTS

- Durham Castle is one of the oldest university buildings in the world, having been integrated into Durham University in 1832.
- The castle was used as a filming location for the Harry Potter series, particularly for scenes set in Hogwarts.
- Durham Castle is home to a large collection of medieval artwork, and the site holds an annual "Castle Lecture" on its history.

NOTEWORTHY SURROUNDINGS

The castle is set in the heart of the historic city of Durham, which is known for its UNESCO-listed cathedral and picturesque medieval streets. The River Wear curves around the city, providing scenic views of the castle from various vantage points. The Durham Botanic Garden and nearby Wharton Park offer lovely spots for walking and exploring. The city itself is a vibrant cultural hub, with many museums, galleries, and theaters.

BAMBURGH CASTLE
NORTHUMBERLAND, ENGLAND

Bamburgh Castle has a rich history that dates back to the 6th century when it was originally the seat of the Kings of Northumbria. The current structure was largely rebuilt in the 12th century following Norman conquest and destruction. Over the centuries, the castle has witnessed invasions, battles, and royal sieges. It was also an important fortress in the defense of northern England during Viking invasions. Today, Bamburgh Castle is a symbol of the Northumberland coast and remains a private residence.

LOCATION

Bamburgh Castle is situated on a dramatic rocky outcrop overlooking the North Sea, in the small village of Bamburgh, Northumberland, in the northeast of England. The location provides breathtaking views of the coast and surrounding countryside.

ARCHITECTURAL FEATURES

The castle is known for its commanding position atop a basalt crag, with a striking curtain wall and imposing towers. Key features include the medieval gatehouse, the Great Hall, and the Inner Ward. The castle's design has been adapted over time to include Victorian renovations, including the addition of elaborate interiors. The walls and towers are still remarkably well-preserved, and the castle is often described as one of the most iconic and picturesque in England.

INTERESTING FACTS

- Bamburgh Castle was the seat of the Kings of Northumbria during the 6th to 9th centuries and has strong historical ties to the early medieval kings and saints of England.
- The castle is often associated with the legendary figure of Sir Lancelot in Arthurian legend, as well as with the Bamburgh Legend
- The castle was extensively restored in the 18th and 19th centuries, largely thanks to the efforts of the Armstrong family, who still own it today.

NOTEWORTHY SURROUNDINGS

The castle offers stunning views of the Northumberland coastline, including the nearby sandy beaches and the Farne Islands. The surrounding area is part of the Northumberland Coast Area of Outstanding Natural Beauty, perfect for walking and nature enthusiasts. Nearby, the picturesque village of Bamburgh is home to traditional stone houses and a charming atmosphere. The nearby town of Alnwick also features the famous Alnwick Castle and gardens.

LEEDS CASTLE
KENT, ENGLAND

HISTORICAL SIGNIFICANCE

Known as "The Loveliest Castle in the World," Leeds Castle has been a royal residence for over 900 years. Originally built in the 12th century, it was the home of several English queens, including Queen Eleanor of Castile, wife of Edward I. The castle was used for a variety of purposes over the centuries, including as a royal residence, a prison, and even as a royal retreat. It played a significant role during the Tudor period, and its long association with English royalty has made it an iconic symbol of the nation's heritage.

LOCATION

Leeds Castle is located in Kent, in the southeast of England, near the village of Leeds, approximately 30 miles from London. The castle is set on an island in a tranquil lake, offering an idyllic setting for visitors to explore.

ARCHITECTURAL FEATURES

The castle's architecture is a blend of medieval and Tudor elements. The main structure is a fortified manor house surrounded by a water-filled moat, giving it a picturesque and serene quality. The castle has been extensively renovated over the years, especially during the Victorian period, when the interiors were transformed into a luxurious private residence. Key features include the Great Hall, a chapel, and the beautifully landscaped gardens.

INTERESTING FACTS

- Leeds Castle was used by six medieval queens of England, including the infamous Queen Catherine of Aragon, first wife of Henry VIII.
- The castle's grounds are home to a maze, which was designed in the 17th century and remains a popular attraction today.
- In the 20th century, the castle was owned by American heiress Olive Willoughby, who made significant improvements to the property, including the creation of the famous "Bird of Prey Centre."

NOTEWORTHY SURROUNDINGS

The castle is set in 500 acres of parkland and gardens, including an award-winning maze, a rose garden, and a medieval-themed woodland area. The surrounding area is rich in natural beauty, with lakes, walking trails, and wildlife. The nearby village of Leeds and the town of Maidstone offer visitors additional historic sites and attractions, including the Kent Life Heritage Farm Park.

WARWICK CASTLE
WARWICKSHIRE, ENGLAND

HISTORICAL SIGNIFICANCE

Warwick Castle was founded by William the Conqueror in 1068 and has since played a crucial role in English history. It was originally built to defend against the Welsh and Scots, and its position on the River Avon made it a strategically important fortification. Over the centuries, the castle was expanded and modernized by various owners, including the Beauchamp and Greville families. During the English Civil War, it was the site of a siege and later became a royal residence. Today, it is one of the most well-preserved medieval castles in England and a major tourist destination.

LOCATION

Warwick Castle is located in the town of Warwick, Warwickshire, in central England. It sits on a bend in the River Avon, offering scenic views of the surrounding countryside and the town itself.

ARCHITECTURAL FEATURES

Warwick Castle's architecture includes a large medieval keep, a gatehouse, and impressive defensive walls. The castle's Great Hall, which was once a banquet hall for royalty, and the towers, including the famous Guy's Tower, are key features. The interior has been beautifully restored to reflect its medieval origins, with tapestries, weaponry, and period furniture. The castle also has extensive grounds with a mound and dungeons.

INTERESTING FACTS

- Warwick Castle is known for its medieval reenactments and live shows, which bring its history to life for visitors.
- The castle has an extensive collection of medieval armor and historical artifacts, which are on display for visitors.
- During the Victorian era, the castle was transformed into a grand residence and included luxurious rooms and gardens.

NOTEWORTHY SURROUNDINGS

Warwick Castle is located in the historic town of Warwick, which is full of charming medieval streets and buildings. The town also has other notable sites, including St. Mary's Church and the Collegiate Church of St. Nicholas. The castle's extensive grounds are perfect for outdoor activities, with lush gardens and a river running through the estate. Nearby, the beautiful Cotswolds region offers additional scenic walks and charming villages to explore.

HAMPTON COURT PALACE
SURREY, ENGLAND

HISTORICAL SIGNIFICANCE

Hampton Court Palace is most famously associated with Henry VIII, who transformed it into a grand royal residence in the 16th century. It was initially built for Cardinal Wolsey, but when Henry VIII fell out of favor with the cardinal, he took over the palace in 1529. Hampton Court played a central role in Tudor history, being the site of many royal events, including Henry's six marriages. The palace also witnessed significant events during the reigns of Elizabeth I, James I, and later monarchs. Today, it remains a symbol of the grandeur and opulence of Tudor England.

LOCATION

Hampton Court Palace is located in Richmond upon Thames, Surrey, approximately 12 miles southwest of central London, situated along the River Thames. Its easy access from London makes it a popular day trip.

ARCHITECTURAL FEATURES

The palace combines Tudor and Baroque architectural styles. Key features include the Tudor Kitchens, the Great Hall (which is one of the largest surviving medieval halls in England), and the ornate Chapel Royal. The Baroque additions made in the 17th century under William III and Mary II include the spectacular Fountain Court and the lavishly designed State Apartments. The palace also boasts magnificent gardens, including the famous Maze and the Formal Gardens with their perfectly manicured hedges.

INTERESTING FACTS

- The palace is one of the best-preserved Tudor buildings in England, with many original rooms still intact.
- Hampton Court is known for its beautiful and expansive gardens, including the oldest surviving hedge maze in the UK.
- The palace also has a connection to the "ghost of Catherine Howard," one of Henry VIII's wives, who is said to haunt the gallery.

NOTEWORTHY SURROUNDINGS

The palace is set in 60 acres of stunning gardens, which include a pond, orchards, a kitchen garden, and the famous Hampton Court Maze. The nearby River Thames offers picturesque views and walking paths, and the surrounding town of Hampton is a charming area with local shops and restaurants. Richmond Park, one of London's largest royal parks, is a short distance away, providing scenic walking and cycling opportunities.

NOTTINGHAM CASTLE
NOTTINGHAM, ENGLAND

Nottingham Castle has a rich history stretching back to the Norman Conquest of 1066. Built by William the Conqueror, the castle was a key stronghold in the center of England, controlling the surrounding area. The castle is most famous for its association with the legend of Robin Hood, as it was the site of the Sheriff of Nottingham's residence. Over the centuries, the castle witnessed many key historical events, including sieges during the English Civil War. The original medieval castle was dismantled in the 17th century, but the castle's legacy endures as an iconic symbol of Nottingham.

LOCATION

Nottingham Castle is located on Castle Rock, a prominent hill in the center of Nottingham, overlooking the city and the surrounding landscape. Its central location provides sweeping views over the city and the Trent Valley.

ARCHITECTURAL FEATURES

While much of the original medieval structure was destroyed, the site features a 17th-century mansion built on the castle's foundations, designed in a classical style by architect Sir Francis Blore. The castle grounds include well-preserved remnants of the castle walls, the ancient gates, and the cave system beneath the hill. The castle's impressive gatehouse is an important surviving feature, as are the gardens and the reconstructed castle's interior, which includes modern museums and galleries.

INTERESTING FACTS

- Nottingham Castle is intrinsically linked with the Robin Hood legends, as it was the residence of the notorious Sheriff of Nottingham.
- The castle was a focal point during the English Civil War, serving as a Royalist stronghold before being besieged and later dismantled.
- The site has recently undergone significant renovations, transforming it into a museum and art gallery showcasing Nottingham's rich history.

NOTEWORTHY SURROUNDINGS

The castle sits within beautiful parkland and gardens, offering visitors an escape from the hustle and bustle of the city. Just a short walk from the castle is the historic Nottingham city center, home to attractions such as the Old Market Square, the Nottingham Contemporary art gallery, and the National Justice Museum. The city's extensive cave system, including the City of Caves attraction, is another intriguing nearby feature.

ROCHESTER CASTLE
KENT, ENGLAND

Rochester Castle, built in the 12th century by the Normans, is one of the best-preserved medieval castles in England. The castle played an important role in the history of the region, serving as a stronghold during the Norman Conquest and later as a royal fortress during the medieval period. It was heavily involved in the conflicts of the 12th century, including the Siege of Rochester Castle in 1215, when it was besieged by King John during the First Barons' War. Despite its heavy fortifications, the castle eventually fell after a prolonged siege.

LOCATION

Rochester Castle is located in the town of Rochester, Kent, southeast of London. It sits on the banks of the River Medway, offering views over the surrounding countryside and the town.

ARCHITECTURAL FEATURES

The most striking feature of Rochester Castle is its massive square keep, which stands 113 feet tall and remains one of the best-preserved keeps in Europe. The keep is surrounded by a large outer bailey and defensive walls. The castle also features remnants of its original moat and a gateway that once provided access to the inner ward. The keep's great hall and other rooms provide a glimpse into medieval life.

INTERESTING FACTS

- The castle's keep, one of the largest in England, is a prime example of Norman military architecture.
- The Siege of Rochester Castle in 1215 is a significant event in English history, as it marked one of the first instances where a castle was besieged using siege engines.
- Rochester Castle has been featured in many films and TV shows due to its well-preserved state and imposing presence.

NOTEWORTHY SURROUNDINGS

The castle is situated in the heart of the historic town of Rochester, which is home to other key landmarks such as Rochester Cathedral and the Dickens Centre, celebrating the town's connection to Charles Dickens. The town also offers scenic riverside walks along the River Medway and a charming high street lined with medieval buildings and independent shops. The nearby Rochester Bridge offers excellent views of the castle and the surrounding area.

ALNWICK CASTLE
NORTHUMBERLAND, ENGLAND

Alnwick Castle has a rich history dating back to the 11th century, when it was built as a fortress to protect the northern border of England. Over the centuries, the castle has been expanded and developed, playing a role in various military conflicts, including the Wars of the Roses. The castle has been the seat of the Percy family, one of the most prominent noble families in England, for over 700 years. The castle has also served as a residence, and today, it remains the home of the Duke of Northumberland.

LOCATION

Alnwick Castle is located in the town of Alnwick, Northumberland, in the northeast of England. It sits on the edge of the Northumberland countryside, with sweeping views of the surrounding farmland and the River Aln.

ARCHITECTURAL FEATURES

Alnwick Castle combines elements of medieval, Renaissance, and Victorian architecture. The most impressive feature is the large keep, surrounded by a defensive wall and a deep moat. The castle also features grand state rooms, including the sumptuous State Drawing Room and the Library, which houses an extensive collection of books and historical artifacts. The castle grounds include beautiful gardens, such as the Poison Garden and the Ornamental Garden, as well as a large, picturesque park.

INTERESTING FACTS

- Alnwick Castle is famous for its role as the location for Hogwarts School of Witchcraft and Wizardry in the Harry Potter films, particularly the scenes of flying lessons on broomsticks.
- The castle also featured in Downton Abbey as the location for various scenes in the series.
- The castle is home to the famous Alnwick Garden, which is renowned for its beautiful plantings and the "Poison Garden," where toxic plants are grown and displayed.

NOTEWORTHY SURROUNDINGS

The castle is set within beautiful parkland, ideal for walking and exploring. The Alnwick Garden is a major attraction, with its themed gardens and fountains. The town of Alnwick itself is a charming market town with a traditional high street, antique shops, and cafes. Just a short distance away is the Northumberland coastline, known for its unspoiled beaches and the nearby Holy Island of Lindisfarne.

HEVER CASTLE
KENT, ENGLAND

HISTORICAL SIGNIFICANCE

Hever Castle is best known as the childhood home of Anne Boleyn, the second wife of Henry VIII and the mother of Queen Elizabeth I. Originally built in the 13th century, the castle became famous when it passed into the Boleyn family in the 15th century. Anne lived there during her youth, and it is believed to be where she spent much of her early life before ascending to the English throne. The castle's historical significance is deeply tied to the Tudor dynasty, as Anne Boleyn's marriage to Henry VIII led to the English Reformation. After Anne's execution in 1536, Hever Castle passed through several hands, including that of Henry VIII, and later, it became the home of the Astor family in the early 20th century.

LOCATION

Hever Castle is located in the village of Hever, in Kent, southeast of London. It is set in a peaceful and rural area, surrounded by the beautiful countryside of Kent.

ARCHITECTURAL FEATURES

The castle is a mix of medieval and Tudor architecture. The main structure includes a 13th-century gatehouse, a series of defensive walls, and a moat. Key architectural features include the Tudor-style interiors, with elegant wood paneling and grand fireplaces, and the atmospheric Long Gallery, which displays portraits of the Boleyn family. The grounds are equally beautiful, featuring formal gardens, a lake, and a yew maze.

INTERESTING FACTS

- Hever Castle has a significant connection to Anne Boleyn, with rooms such as the Boleyn Room and the Anne Boleyn exhibition providing a detailed look at her life.
- The castle has been in the possession of several prominent families, including the Astors, who restored and renovated the castle in the early 20th century.
- The castle is home to a large collection of Tudor memorabilia, including a rare portrait of Anne Boleyn.

NOTEWORTHY SURROUNDINGS

The castle is surrounded by stunning gardens, including a rose garden, Italian Garden, and an expansive lake. The grounds are perfect for leisurely strolls, with picturesque views of the Kent countryside. The nearby village of Hever is charming, and the area is part of the High Weald Area of Outstanding Natural Beauty. Nearby attractions include the historic town of Tunbridge Wells and the rolling hills of the Kent Downs.

CAERNARFON CASTLE
WALES

HISTORICAL SIGNIFICANCE

Caernarfon Castle is one of the most iconic castles in Wales, famous for its imposing size and dramatic location. Built by Edward I during his conquest of Wales in the late 13th century, the castle was designed to be a symbol of English dominance over the Welsh. It was also the site of the investiture of the Prince of Wales, a role that continues today with the British heir to the throne. Caernarfon Castle is a UNESCO World Heritage site and one of the most important medieval fortresses in Europe. Its design, inspired by the walls of Constantinople, is a stunning example of military architecture.

LOCATION

Caernarfon Castle is located in the town of Caernarfon, in Gwynedd, North Wales. It sits on the edge of the Menai Strait, with panoramic views over the water to the island of Anglesey.

ARCHITECTURAL FEATURES

The castle is renowned for its distinct and impressive medieval design, with polygonal towers and a series of defensive walls. The walls are reinforced with formidable battlements, and the massive Eagle Tower is the centerpiece, offering stunning views of the surrounding area. Inside, the castle contains a collection of rooms that showcase its historical importance, including the Great Hall, the Royal Apartments, and various chambers. The castle's outer walls were constructed using a combination of stone and mortar.

INTERESTING FACTS

- Caernarfon Castle is famous for being the site where the Prince of Wales has been invested, with the most recent being Prince Charles in 1969.
- The castle's design was inspired by the Byzantine Empire and the ancient walls of Constantinople.
- The castle played a major role in the suppression of Welsh uprisings, especially during the late 13th and early 14th centuries.

NOTEWORTHY SURROUNDINGS

The castle is situated along the Menai Strait, with beautiful views across the water. The surrounding town of Caernarfon is a historic market town with narrow streets, medieval buildings, and a lively atmosphere. Just to the north, the stunning Snowdonia National Park offers a wealth of outdoor activities, including hiking and nature trails. The nearby Anglesey Island, accessible via the Menai Suspension Bridge, offers charming beaches and coastal paths.

CONWY CASTLE
WALES

HISTORICAL SIGNIFICANCE

Conwy Castle is another UNESCO World Heritage site built by Edward I as part of his campaign to subdue Wales in the 13th century. The castle's construction was part of a series of fortresses along the north Welsh coast designed to maintain English control over Wales. Conwy Castle played an important role in the Wars of Welsh Independence, especially during the rebellion of Llywelyn the Last. The castle's construction was highly advanced for its time, and it was one of the most powerful military fortifications in medieval Wales.

LOCATION

Conwy Castle is located in the town of Conwy, North Wales, positioned strategically on the banks of the River Conwy, with breathtaking views of Snowdonia National Park in the distance.

ARCHITECTURAL FEATURES

The castle's design is a masterpiece of medieval military engineering, with eight massive towers and a system of defensive walls that encircle the town of Conwy. The castle's walls and gates are exceptionally well-preserved, and its towers offer spectacular views of the surrounding area. Inside, visitors can explore the Great Hall, the King's Chamber, and the battlements. Conwy Castle is renowned for its well-preserved state and is one of the most complete castles in Britain.

INTERESTING FACTS

- Conwy Castle was a key component in Edward I's "Iron Ring" of fortresses built to subdue Wales during his conquest.
- The castle has been used in several films and TV shows, including The Eagle and The Lion in Winter.
- The town of Conwy, with its well-preserved medieval walls, is also part of the UNESCO World Heritage site, making it one of the best-preserved examples of a medieval walled town in the UK.

NOTEWORTHY SURROUNDINGS

The castle is surrounded by the beautiful scenery of Conwy and the surrounding Snowdonia National Park, which is a haven for outdoor enthusiasts. The town of Conwy itself is full of history, with its well-preserved medieval walls, the smallest house in Britain, and the charming quay. The nearby town of Llandudno offers a classic Victorian seaside experience, and the picturesque Bodnant Garden, one of the UK's finest, is located nearby.

TINTAGEL CASTLE
CORNWALL, ENGLAND

HISTORICAL SIGNIFICANCE

Tintagel Castle is steeped in legend and history, most famously associated with the myth of King Arthur. According to medieval legend, Tintagel is the birthplace of King Arthur, where he was conceived by Uther Pendragon and Igraine. The site has been a place of mythological and historical importance for centuries. Archaeological evidence suggests the site was an important settlement during the 5th and 6th centuries, with links to both Roman and early medieval Britain. While its connection to the Arthurian legend is uncertain, Tintagel's dramatic location and ancient ruins continue to captivate visitors.

LOCATION

Tintagel Castle is located on the rugged north coast of Cornwall, perched dramatically on a clifftop above the Atlantic Ocean. The site offers breathtaking views of the coastline and is a popular destination for those exploring Cornwall's coastal beauty.

ARCHITECTURAL FEATURES

Tintagel Castle consists of a complex of ruins, with the most impressive feature being its location on the clifftop. The castle's remains include the ruins of a large courtyard, a chapel, and a series of walls and gateways that hint at the size and importance of the site. The surrounding cliffs, accessed via a bridge to the mainland, enhance the site's dramatic appeal. Archaeological excavations have uncovered pottery, coins, and other artifacts that provide insight into its history.

INTERESTING FACTS

- Tintagel Castle is closely linked to the legend of King Arthur and has been a significant location for Arthurian enthusiasts and scholars.
- The site has been the subject of ongoing archaeological digs, revealing evidence of a settlement dating back to the 5th and 6th centuries.
- A new footbridge was constructed in 2019 to provide better access to the castle from the mainland, enhancing the experience for visitors.

NOTEWORTHY SURROUNDINGS

The castle's dramatic clifftop setting is part of the stunning Tintagel Head, which offers panoramic views of the Atlantic Ocean. The surrounding area is part of the Cornwall Area of Outstanding Natural Beauty, with rugged coastlines, beaches, and coastal walking trails. The village of Tintagel nearby is home to charming shops and cafes. The Tintagel Old Post Office, a 14th-century building, is another local landmark, and the nearby St. Materiana's Church.

CASTLE RISING
NORFOLK, ENGLAND

Castle Rising is one of the most well-preserved early medieval castles in England, with a history dating back to the Norman period. Built around 1138 by the powerful de Warrenne family, the castle played a significant role in medieval England. It became a royal residence in the 14th century when it was used as a prison for Queen Isabella, the widow of Edward II, after her involvement in the deposition of her husband. The castle's strategic location and its role in the turbulent politics of medieval England make it an important site in the nation's history.

LOCATION

Castle Rising is located in the village of Castle Rising, near King's Lynn in Norfolk, Eastern England. It is set in a picturesque rural location, surrounded by the flat fenland landscape of the region.

ARCHITECTURAL FEATURES

The most striking feature of Castle Rising is its massive keep, which is one of the largest in England. The keep is built on a raised mound, providing a commanding view of the surrounding area. The castle's walls are made of flint and limestone, and it was once surrounded by a deep ditch or moat, parts of which are still visible today. The keep is rectangular in shape, with four corner towers and thick defensive walls. The interior of the keep contains a series of vaulted chambers and a large hall, where significant events were once held.

INTERESTING FACTS

- Castle Rising is famous for its impressive state of preservation, particularly its massive keep, which remains largely intact despite its age.
- Queen Isabella, known for her role in the overthrow of her husband, King Edward II, was imprisoned here in the 14th century, adding a dramatic personal history to the castle.
- The castle was largely abandoned as a military fortification by the 16th century and was converted into a private residence.

NOTEWORTHY SURROUNDINGS

The village of Castle Rising is a charming, peaceful location, with the castle being the primary historical landmark. Nearby, the town of King's Lynn offers additional historical attractions and the beautiful countryside of Norfolk. The surrounding area is rich in natural beauty, perfect for walking, and there are several nearby coastal sites to explore, including the sand dunes of Heacham and the Norfolk Coast Area of Outstanding Natural Beauty.

SHERBORNE CASTLE
DORSET, ENGLAND

HISTORICAL SIGNIFICANCE

Sherborne Castle, located in Dorset, was originally built in the 12th century as a fortress and royal residence, but it was transformed into a beautiful stately home in the 16th century. It was the seat of the Digby family for centuries, and it played an important role in the English Civil War, when it was briefly held by Royalist forces. The castle's transformation into a Renaissance-style mansion was commissioned by Sir Walter Raleigh in the late 1500s. Sherborne Castle is one of the finest examples of a country house in England.

LOCATION

Sherborne Castle is located just outside the town of Sherborne in Dorset, in the South West of England. The castle is set in a picturesque landscape, surrounded by beautiful parkland and the stunning Sherborne Lake.

ARCHITECTURAL FEATURES

The castle is a striking example of Renaissance architecture, featuring a mix of Tudor and Elizabethan elements. The grandiose building has large, symmetrical windows, extensive use of brick and stone, and a beautiful interior with richly decorated rooms. The central part of the building is the oldest, dating back to the 12th century, and features a large, elegant Great Hall. The addition of the Renaissance-style gardens, lake, and surrounding parkland by Sir Walter Raleigh adds to the aesthetic charm of the estate.

INTERESTING FACTS

- Sir Walter Raleigh, the famous explorer, was instrumental in transforming Sherborne Castle into a grand mansion in the late 1500s.
- The castle was used as a Royalist stronghold during the English Civil War before being taken by Parliamentarian forces.
- The estate is home to one of the finest landscaped gardens in England, designed by Capability Brown in the 18th century.

NOTEWORTHY SURROUNDINGS

Sherborne Castle is set within a 1,000-acre estate, with breathtaking views of the surrounding Dorset countryside. The beautiful Sherborne Lake, which the castle overlooks, is perfect for leisurely walks or boat trips. The nearby town of Sherborne is known for its historic abbey and charming streets, with independent shops, cafes, and historical buildings, including the Sherborne School, one of England's oldest and most prestigious schools.

CHESTER CASTLE
CHESHIRE, ENGLAND

HISTORICAL SIGNIFICANCE

Chester Castle has a long and varied history, dating back to the Roman era. Originally established as a Roman fort, the site was later used by the Normans after the 1066 Conquest to build a motte-and-bailey castle. The castle's keep was built in the 12th century and was a key part of Chester's defense system. It has seen many significant events throughout English history, including the English Civil War, when it was heavily involved in military activities. The castle's strategic location, overlooking the River Dee and the city of Chester, was vital for controlling the area.

LOCATION

Chester Castle is located in the city of Chester, in Cheshire, North West England. It stands on a sandstone hill, offering panoramic views of the city, the River Dee, and the surrounding countryside.

ARCHITECTURAL FEATURES

The castle consists of both Roman and medieval elements, with the most significant feature being its Norman keep. The keep is square, with thick defensive walls, a large central courtyard, and a series of impressive towers. The walls are reinforced by a Roman fort's remains, which still can be seen at the site. The castle also features a large gatehouse and an entrance that was once heavily fortified. The interior contains several rooms and chambers, including a medieval Great Hall and a ceremonial room.

INTERESTING FACTS

- Chester Castle was originally a Roman military fort, later becoming a major Norman stronghold after 1066.
- The castle's keep has survived largely intact, making it one of the best-preserved examples of Norman architecture in the UK.
- The castle played a key role during the English Civil War, with its fortifications being used by both Royalists and Parliamentarians.

NOTEWORTHY SURROUNDINGS

The castle is located in the heart of Chester, a city famous for its medieval history and Roman heritage. Chester's well-preserved city walls, Roman amphitheater, and the distinctive black-and-white timber-framed buildings are key features of the city. The River Dee,, provides beautiful riverside walks, and nearby Grosvenor Park offers tranquil green space with views over the castle. The Chester Zoo and the Chester Cathedral are also major attractions in the city.

PENDENNIS CASTLE
CORNWALL, ENGLAND

Pendennis Castle, built by Henry VIII between 1540 and 1545, was part of a chain of coastal defenses constructed to protect England from potential invasion by the French and Spanish during the 16th century. The castle played a vital role during the English Civil War, being a Royalist stronghold in Cornwall, and withstood a lengthy siege in 1646 before surrendering to Parliamentarian forces. Pendennis was also used during both World Wars as a coastal defense and has remained a prominent feature of Cornwall's military history.

LOCATION

Pendennis Castle is located in Falmouth, Cornwall, on a headland overlooking the entrance to the Fal Estuary. Its position provides commanding views over the coastline and the sea, making it an ideal location for defense.

ARCHITECTURAL FEATURES

Pendennis Castle is a coastal fortress with a distinctive circular keep and thick defensive walls. The castle was designed with multiple layers of fortifications, including a series of gun emplacements and ramparts. The keep is equipped with a large central courtyard and has a series of rooms that were used for military and royal purposes. In addition to its military defenses, Pendennis features a lighthouse and several 19th and 20th-century additions, including a battery of coastal artillery.

INTERESTING FACTS

- Pendennis Castle is one of the best-preserved Tudor coastal fortresses in England.
- The castle withstood a siege during the English Civil War when Royalist forces held the fort for several months against the Parliamentarians.
- Pendennis was used during both World Wars as part of the coastal defense network to protect against German invasion.

NOTEWORTHY SURROUNDINGS

Pendennis Castle sits on a scenic headland with stunning views of Falmouth Bay, the Fal Estuary, and the surrounding coastline. The area is rich in maritime history, and the nearby town of Falmouth is a hub for boaters and sailors, with a vibrant harbor and maritime museum. The castle is surrounded by beautiful gardens and walking trails, including paths that lead to the nearby Gyllyngvase Beach and the picturesque countryside of Cornwall.

LULWORTH CASTLE
DORSET, ENGLAND

Lulworth Castle, located in Dorset, is a beautiful country house that was built in the early 17th century on the site of an earlier medieval castle. The original medieval structure, which dates back to the 12th century, was likely a fortress built by the de Lulworth family. However, the current castle was constructed between 1609 and 1610 by Thomas Howard, the 3rd Earl of Suffolk, as a hunting lodge and country residence. Over the years, Lulworth Castle has passed through several hands and has been modified and renovated. Though not used as a military stronghold, it still holds significant historical value as an example of early modern castle architecture.

LOCATION

Lulworth Castle is situated in the Lulworth Estate near the village of West Lulworth, in Dorset, on the south coast of England. The estate is located within the stunning Lulworth Cove area, close to the Jurassic Coast, a UNESCO World Heritage site.

ARCHITECTURAL FEATURES

Lulworth Castle is an intriguing blend of Renaissance and medieval design. The main structure is a large square building with a central dome, which was unusual for the time and provides an elegant country house feel. The original medieval castle walls can still be seen in parts of the estate, though much of the medieval fortress was demolished during the early construction of the house. The interior features a series of grand rooms, while the surrounding parkland contains formal gardens, a lake, and wooded areas.

INTERESTING FACTS

- Lulworth Castle is often considered a "folly" due to its picturesque, somewhat whimsical design, which contrasts with the typical fortifications of earlier castles.
- The castle's chapel contains the tomb of the 3rd Earl of Suffolk and his wife.
- The castle was used as a hunting lodge for the Howard family and remains a stunning example of a country house from the early 17th century.

NOTEWORTHY SURROUNDINGS

Lulworth Castle is set within a vast estate, with its grounds offering beautiful walking paths and views of the surrounding Dorset countryside. The estate is located near Lulworth Cove, famous for its scenic natural beauty and limestone rock formations. The nearby Durdle Door, a natural limestone arch on the coast, adds to the area's dramatic landscapes. The Jurassic Coast is renowned for its rich history and fossil finds.

BODIAM CASTLE
EAST SUSSEX, ENGLAND

Bodiam Castle is one of the most iconic and picturesque medieval castles in England. Built in 1385 by Sir Edward Dalyngrigge, a former knight of Edward III, Bodiam Castle was designed as a defensive fortress to protect the region from French invaders during the Hundred Years' War. The castle is notable for its near-perfect preservation and its location on a large moat, which gives it a fairy-tale appearance. While never involved in any significant military action, Bodiam Castle played an important role in the defensive network of southeast England.

LOCATION

Bodiam Castle is located in East Sussex, near the village of Bodiam. It is set in the beautiful countryside, surrounded by a deep moat and overlooking the River Rother. The location provides stunning views of the surrounding landscape, which includes wetlands, forests, and rolling hills.

ARCHITECTURAL FEATURES

Bodiam Castle is renowned for its classic medieval design, featuring a rectangular layout with four corner towers and a central courtyard. The castle is surrounded by a wide, deep moat, which gives it a distinctive, almost magical appearance. The castle's walls are made of stone, and the towers are punctuated by crenellated battlements. The interior contains a Great Hall, a chapel, and several chambers, though much of the original interior has been lost over time.

INTERESTING FACTS

- Bodiam Castle is often considered one of the most photogenic castles in England due to its picturesque setting and dramatic silhouette against the moat.
- The castle was built with a focus on defensive features, including its extensive moat, drawbridge, and high walls.
- The castle was used for agricultural purposes in the 18th century, and later it was restored in the 19th century by Sir Henry Angell, who sought to preserve its medieval charm.

NOTEWORTHY SURROUNDINGS

The castle's moat and surrounding wetlands are home to a variety of wildlife, including birds and aquatic life. The nearby village of Bodiam is charming, and the surrounding East Sussex countryside offers a wealth of outdoor activities, including walking, cycling, and nature observation. The area is also close to the High Weald Area of Outstanding Natural Beauty and several historical sites, including the town of Hastings, which is known for the Battle of Hastings in 1066.

WARKWORTH CASTLE
NORTHUMBERLAND, ENGLAND

Warkworth Castle is a historic fortress with a rich and varied history. The castle was founded in the 12th century, likely by the powerful de Muschamp family, and later became the seat of the Percy family, one of the most influential noble families in England. The castle's strategic location on a hill overlooking the River Coquet allowed it to play an important role in both local defense and regional politics. It was a key stronghold during the Wars of the Roses, and its significance grew during the medieval period, though it was eventually abandoned in the 17th century.

LOCATION

Warkworth Castle is located in the village of Warkworth, Northumberland, in the northeast of England. The castle is perched on a natural hilltop with commanding views of the surrounding countryside and the River Coquet.

ARCHITECTURAL FEATURES

Warkworth Castle is known for its impressive ruins, which include a large, well-preserved keep and the remains of a surrounding curtain wall. The castle is a mixture of Norman and medieval architecture, with an iconic round keep, crenellated walls, and large defensive towers. The interior contains the remains of a Great Hall, kitchens, and living quarters, while the surrounding battlements offer expansive views of the river and landscape. The castle's location and architecture make it a fine example of medieval fortifications.

INTERESTING FACTS

- Warkworth Castle was the seat of the Percy family for centuries, including during the time of Henry Percy, known as Hotspur, who was a prominent figure in English history and involved in the Wars of the Roses.
- The castle's location on a hill provided it with strong defensive advantages, making it an important military site.
- The Percy family's coat of arms is still displayed within the ruins of the castle, signifying its long association with the powerful family.

NOTEWORTHY SURROUNDINGS

Warkworth Castle is located within the charming village of Warkworth, which has a quaint high street with shops, pubs, and cafes. The surrounding countryside is ideal for walking, with trails that offer views of the river and the castle ruins. Warkworth is close to the Northumberland Coast Area of Outstanding Natural Beauty, known for its beautiful beaches and historic sites, including Alnwick Castle, which is just a short drive away.

PEVERIL CASTLE
DERBYSHIRE, ENGLAND

HISTORICAL SIGNIFICANCE

Peveril Castle is one of the earliest Norman castles built after the Conquest of 1066, established by William Peverel, a trusted follower of William the Conqueror. The castle was strategically placed on a hill above the village of Castleton, providing a commanding view of the surrounding Peak District. While it never saw significant military action, Peveril Castle played an important role in regional governance. The castle is most notable for its association with the medieval kings of England, as it was one of the royal castles controlled by the Crown.

LOCATION

Peveril Castle is located in the village of Castleton, in the Peak District National Park, Derbyshire, in central England. The castle is set on a prominent hilltop, offering panoramic views of the surrounding valley and dramatic landscapes of the Peak District.

ARCHITECTURAL FEATURES

Peveril Castle is a ruined Norman fortification, with its most prominent feature being the large keep, which is still partially intact. The castle's layout consists of a motte (a raised earth mound) with a bailey (enclosed courtyard) and a keep at the top. The keep was originally rectangular, with thick defensive walls. The remains of the gatehouse, the foundations of the bailey, and parts of the castle walls are still visible today. The castle was constructed using local stone and was designed to be a stronghold to protect the region.

INTERESTING FACTS

- Peveril Castle is one of the earliest Norman castles in England, dating back to the 12th century.
- The castle's location on a hill made it an ideal defensive position, with views over the valley of Castleton and the surrounding area.
- The castle has been in a state of ruin for centuries, but it remains a popular tourist destination due to its historical significance and scenic views.

NOTEWORTHY SURROUNDINGS

The castle is located in the picturesque village of Castleton, a popular tourist destination known for its caves, including the famous Blue John Cavern, and its proximity to the stunning landscapes of the Peak District National Park. The area offers excellent hiking opportunities, with trails leading to the castle and surrounding natural features such as Mam Tor, known as the "Shivering Mountain," and the rugged terrain of the Hope Valley.

FOTHERINGHAY CASTLE
NORTHAMPTONSHIRE, ENGLAND

Fotheringhay Castle, located in Northamptonshire, is one of England's most historically significant castle sites. It is famously known as the birthplace of Richard III, the last Plantagenet king of England, who was born here in 1452. The castle also has strong connections to the Tudor dynasty; it was at Fotheringhay Castle that Mary, Queen of Scots, was tried and executed in 1587. The castle played a role in the Wars of the Roses, and after Richard III's death, the site became a symbol of the tumultuous period of English history.

LOCATION

Fotheringhay Castle is located in the village of Fotheringhay, near Peterborough, in Northamptonshire, East England. The site is set on the banks of the River Nene, offering scenic views over the surrounding countryside.

ARCHITECTURAL FEATURES

The original structure of Fotheringhay Castle was a large motte-and-bailey castle, later expanded into a fortified residence. The most prominent feature of the castle was its massive keep, which stood on a raised mound. Little of the original castle remains today, as much of it was demolished in the 17th century, but the site's earthworks and the foundations of the keep are still visible. The castle once had a large outer bailey, defensive walls, and several towers, which would have made it a formidable fortress in its day.

INTERESTING FACTS

- Fotheringhay Castle was the birthplace of Richard III, who was the last English king to die in battle, at the Battle of Bosworth Field in 1485.
- The castle is famously linked to the tragic fate of Mary, Queen of Scots, who was executed here after being convicted of plotting to assassinate Queen Elizabeth I.
- The castle was largely dismantled after the English Civil War, and much of the stone was repurposed for other buildings.

NOTEWORTHY SURROUNDINGS

The site of Fotheringhay Castle is now a peaceful rural location, with the village of Fotheringhay offering a charming setting. The River Nene runs nearby, providing scenic views and walking paths. The nearby town of Peterborough is home to Peterborough Cathedral, a notable example of medieval architecture. The surrounding countryside of Northamptonshire offers various walking routes, perfect for those exploring England's rich history.

OXFORD CASTLE
OXFORD, ENGLAND

HISTORICAL SIGNIFICANCE

Oxford Castle is a Norman fortress that dates back to the 11th century, making it one of the oldest castles in England. Originally built to establish Norman control over Oxford, the castle has seen centuries of development and change. It played a key role in England's military history during the medieval period and was used as a royal residence. Over time, it became a prison, and the castle's notorious prison complex was in use until the 1990s. Oxford Castle is also closely associated with the rise of the University of Oxford, which eventually overtook the castle's role as the city's center of power.

LOCATION

Oxford Castle is situated in the heart of Oxford, one of the world's oldest university towns. The castle is located near the River Thames, surrounded by the historic center of the city and the University of Oxford's colleges.

ARCHITECTURAL FEATURES

Oxford Castle is known for its impressive medieval architecture, with its central feature being the 11th-century motte-and-bailey structure. The site includes the original motte, which offers panoramic views of Oxford, as well as a large keep built later in the 12th century. Over time, the castle was modified into a prison, and remnants of the prison's cells and buildings can still be seen today. The Castle's St. George's Tower, the only surviving part of the medieval structure, offers spectacular views of Oxford.

INTERESTING FACTS

- Oxford Castle was originally built by the Norman conqueror Robert d'Oilly in 1071 to secure the city after the Norman Conquest.
- The castle was later used as a prison for several centuries, and one of its most famous prisoners was the highwayman Dick Turpin.
- Oxford Castle is part of the Oxford Heritage Trail, a popular tourist route that explores the city's rich history and landmarks.

NOTEWORTHY SURROUNDINGS

Oxford Castle is located in the heart of Oxford, where visitors can explore numerous historical sites, including the University of Oxford, the Bodleian Library, and the Ashmolean Museum. The city itself is rich in medieval and Georgian architecture. The nearby Oxford Botanic Garden provides a tranquil space, and the River Thames offers scenic walks along its banks. The famous colleges of Oxford University, are just a short distance away.

TATTERSHALL CASTLE
LINCOLNSHIRE, ENGLAND

HISTORICAL SIGNIFICANCE

Tattershall Castle, located in Lincolnshire, is a remarkable example of a 15th-century red-brick castle. It was built by Lord Ralph Cromwell, a key figure in the court of Henry VI, and is famous for its distinctive architecture and its connection to the Cromwell family. The castle played a significant role in English noble life during the late medieval period, and its design was intended not only as a fortress but also as a symbol of wealth and power. The castle's red-brick construction is unusual for the time, making it a significant example of late medieval architecture.

LOCATION

Tattershall Castle is located near the village of Tattershall, in Lincolnshire, East England. The castle is set on a large estate with beautiful parkland, lakes, and gardens, providing a tranquil atmosphere in the heart of the Lincolnshire countryside.

ARCHITECTURAL FEATURES

Tattershall Castle is built primarily from red brick, which gives it a striking appearance compared to many other stone-built castles of the time. The castle has a central tower (keep), which rises dramatically above the surrounding landscape. The keep features a grand staircase and a series of ornate rooms and chambers. The castle also has a large, decorative gatehouse, a defensive courtyard, and an impressive series of towers and battlements.

INTERESTING FACTS

- Tattershall Castle is an early example of brick-built architecture, which was rare in England during the 15th century.
- It was home to the influential Cromwell family, who played a key role in English politics during the reign of Henry VI and beyond.
- The castle is a Grade I listed building, recognized for its exceptional historical and architectural importance.

NOTEWORTHY SURROUNDINGS

Tattershall Castle is located in a picturesque setting, surrounded by tranquil parkland, lakes, and gardens, making it ideal for outdoor activities such as walking and picnicking. The nearby Tattershall Lakes provide opportunities for boating and fishing. Lincoln, the county town of Lincolnshire, is a short drive away, where visitors can explore the stunning Lincoln Cathedral, Lincoln Castle, and the charming medieval streets of the city.

HURST CASTLE
HAMPSHIRE, ENGLAND

Hurst Castle is a coastal fortress located on a narrow spit of land on the Solent, the strait separating the Isle of Wight from mainland England. Built by Henry VIII in the 1540s, it was part of his system of coastal defenses designed to protect England from potential invasion during the period of conflict with France and Spain. The castle played a role in the English Civil War and was later adapted for use in both World Wars. It also served as a prison for German soldiers during World War I and II, adding to its diverse military history.

LOCATION

Hurst Castle is located on Hurst Spit, a long narrow stretch of land that extends into the Solent, near the village of Keyhaven in Hampshire. The castle is surrounded by beautiful views of the sea, the Isle of Wight, and the New Forest.

ARCHITECTURAL FEATURES

Hurst Castle was originally constructed as a coastal artillery fort and has a distinctive Tudor design with a large central block and defensive walls. The castle was later expanded and modified, particularly during the 19th century when additional gun emplacements and barracks were added. The structure includes a central keep, a series of ramparts, and large gun platforms designed to protect the Solent and the southern coast of England. The castle also has a lighthouse, which was added in the 19th century.

INTERESTING FACTS

- Hurst Castle was originally built by Henry VIII to defend against French and Spanish invasions during the 16th century.
- The castle was equipped with heavy artillery during both World Wars, serving as a coastal defense installation and military post.
- The castle is now a popular visitor attraction, offering tours that delve into its rich military history.

NOTEWORTHY SURROUNDINGS

Hurst Castle is surrounded by beautiful landscapes, with views over the Solent and the Isle of Wight. The area is part of the New Forest National Park, known for its ancient woodlands, heathlands, and wild ponies. The village of Keyhaven offers scenic walking paths and access to Hurst Spit, where visitors can explore the coastal environment and enjoy stunning sea views.

CHIRK CASTLE
WALES

Chirk Castle, located in North Wales, is one of the best-preserved medieval fortresses in the region. It was built in the late 13th century by Edward I as part of his campaign to secure his rule over Wales. The castle is strategically positioned near the Welsh-English border, making it a key military stronghold during the medieval period. It was also a residence for the influential Salusbury family, whose descendants still live in the castle today. Chirk Castle has witnessed numerous changes over the centuries, but its history remains deeply connected to Welsh and English power struggles.

LOCATION

Chirk Castle is situated near the village of Chirk, in the Wrexham area of North Wales. It is set on a hilltop overlooking the beautiful Ceiriog Valley and is close to the border with England. The castle's position provides commanding views of the surrounding landscape.

ARCHITECTURAL FEATURES

Chirk Castle is an excellent example of a medieval fortress, with thick stone walls, four corner towers, and a central keep. The castle's design is typical of Edward I's fortifications in Wales, featuring defensive elements like a moat and a drawbridge. Over the centuries, the castle has been expanded and renovated, and it now features beautiful interiors that blend medieval and early modern designs. The surrounding grounds are also beautifully landscaped, with formal gardens, wooded areas, and a 19th-century pleasure ground.

INTERESTING FACTS

- Chirk Castle was built between 1295 and 1310 by Edward I as part of his efforts to control the region during his conquest of Wales.
- The castle remains one of the best-preserved medieval castles in Wales and is still lived in by the descendants of the Salusbury family.
- It is now managed by the National Trust and is open to the public for tours, allowing visitors to explore its historic interiors and extensive grounds.

NOTEWORTHY SURROUNDINGS

Chirk Castle is set in picturesque surroundings, with the castle's hilltop location offering stunning views of the nearby valleys and forests. The castle is surrounded by extensive gardens, which include both formal and informal sections. The nearby town of Llangollen, famous for its beautiful setting by the River Dee, is only a short drive away and offers additional scenic walks and cultural attractions. The surrounding area is also popular for hiking in the Berwyn Mountains.

BOLTON CASTLE
NORTH YORKSHIRE, ENGLAND

Bolton Castle, located in North Yorkshire, is a 14th-century medieval fortress that has played a pivotal role in English history. It was built by Richard le Scrope, a powerful nobleman, and has witnessed several key events throughout its long history. The castle is most famous for its role in the imprisonment of Mary, Queen of Scots, who was held here for several months in the late 16th century. The castle also played a role during the English Civil War, as it was held by Royalists before being besieged by Parliamentary forces.

LOCATION

Bolton Castle is located in the village of Bolton, near the town of Leyburn, in the Yorkshire Dales, North Yorkshire. It sits in a remote, scenic part of the Yorkshire Dales National Park, surrounded by stunning countryside.

ARCHITECTURAL FEATURES

Bolton Castle is a quintessential example of a medieval fortress, with a large rectangular keep at its core. The castle features four corner towers, a fortified gatehouse, and a defensive courtyard. The exterior walls of the castle remain remarkably intact, while the interiors have been preserved and restored to reflect its history. The castle's well-maintained grounds include gardens, orchards, and a labyrinth of walking paths.

INTERESTING FACTS

- Bolton Castle was once home to the Scrope family and is best known for being the prison of Mary, Queen of Scots, who was held there for six months in 1568.
- The castle is one of the few in England to still have its roof intact, which adds to its authenticity and makes it a popular tourist destination.
- It was heavily involved in the English Civil War, when it was besieged by Parliamentary forces in 1645.

NOTEWORTHY SURROUNDINGS

Bolton Castle is situated in the heart of the Yorkshire Dales, a region known for its stunning natural beauty. The surrounding area is perfect for outdoor activities such as hiking, cycling, and birdwatching. The nearby village of Leyburn offers traditional Yorkshire charm and provides access to various walking trails. The nearby Aysgarth Falls, a series of stunning waterfalls in the Yorkshire Dales, are also a popular natural attraction.

EDINBURGH CASTLE
EDINBURGH, SCOTLAND

HISTORICAL SIGNIFICANCE

Edinburgh Castle is one of Scotland's most iconic landmarks and a symbol of Scottish history and heritage. Sitting atop Castle Rock, an extinct volcano, the castle has been a key military stronghold for centuries and played a central role in numerous battles. It was the royal residence of Scottish kings and queens, including Mary, Queen of Scots, who gave birth to James VI of Scotland (and later James I of England) within the castle. The castle has witnessed pivotal moments in Scottish history, including the Wars of Scottish Independence and the Jacobite uprisings.

LOCATION

Edinburgh Castle is located in the heart of Edinburgh, Scotland's capital city. The castle sits dramatically on Castle Rock, offering panoramic views of the surrounding city and the extinct volcano Arthur's Seat. Its central location makes it easily accessible from Edinburgh's Old Town.

ARCHITECTURAL FEATURES

Edinburgh Castle is a stunning example of Scottish military architecture, with its formidable defensive walls and towers. The castle features several key buildings, including St. Margaret's Chapel (the oldest surviving building in Edinburgh), the Royal Palace, and the Crown Jewels of Scotland. The castle complex is dominated by the Great Hall and the iconic Mons Meg, an enormous medieval cannon. The castle's strategic location on Castle Rock makes it virtually impregnable, with sheer cliffs on all sides.

INTERESTING FACTS

- Edinburgh Castle is home to the Crown Jewels of Scotland, including the Stone of Destiny, which is used in the coronation of Scottish monarchs.
- The castle has been a royal residence for over a thousand years and is one of Scotland's most important cultural and historic sites.
- The castle has been the setting for many important events in Scottish history, including the coronation of Mary, Queen of Scots, and the defense against English invasions.

NOTEWORTHY SURROUNDINGS

Edinburgh Castle is located in the heart of Edinburgh, close to many of the city's key attractions, including the Royal Mile, the Palace of Holyroodhouse, and the National Museum of Scotland. The castle itself offers breathtaking views of the city and the surrounding landscape, including the extinct volcano Arthur's Seat. Visitors can explore the cobbled streets of Edinburgh's Old Town, which is a UNESCO World Heritage site.

STIRLING CASTLE
STIRLING, SCOTLAND

HISTORICAL SIGNIFICANCE

Stirling Castle is one of Scotland's most historically significant castles, playing a central role in the country's history. It has been the site of several key battles in Scotland's Wars of Independence, including the Battle of Stirling Bridge in 1297, where William Wallace famously defeated the English forces. The castle was also a royal residence, particularly for the Stewart kings and queens, including Mary, Queen of Scots. Stirling Castle has long been a symbol of Scottish strength and resistance, and it is intimately tied to Scotland's struggle for independence.

LOCATION

Stirling Castle is located in the town of Stirling, in central Scotland, on a volcanic rock outcrop that offers commanding views over the surrounding area. It is strategically positioned between the Scottish Highlands and the Lowlands, making it an important military stronghold throughout Scottish history.

ARCHITECTURAL FEATURES

Stirling Castle is an excellent example of Renaissance and medieval Scottish architecture. The castle features a royal palace, a great hall, and several defensive towers. The castle's most distinctive feature is its elegant Renaissance design, including the extensive use of decorative stonework and impressive vaulted ceilings. Stirling Castle also has a number of well-preserved structures, including the Stirling Castle Chapel and the Great Hall, which are significant examples of medieval and Renaissance architecture.

INTERESTING FACTS

- Stirling Castle was the site of the Battle of Stirling Bridge, where William Wallace and Andrew Moray defeated the English in 1297.
- The castle was a key residence for Scottish kings and queens, including James VI of Scotland (who became James I of England).
- The castle is closely associated with the reign of Mary, Queen of Scots, who was crowned queen at the castle in 1543.

NOTEWORTHY SURROUNDINGS

Stirling Castle is situated within the town of Stirling, which is home to several other historical attractions, including the Wallace Monument, dedicated to William Wallace, and the Battle of Stirling Bridge site. The castle offers stunning views of the surrounding countryside, including the River Forth and the nearby Ochil Hills. The town of Stirling itself is rich in history and offers plenty of shops, restaurants, and cultural experiences.

URQUHARTCASTLE
LOCH NESS, SCOTLAND

Urquhart Castle is a historic fortress located on the western shores of Loch Ness in the Scottish Highlands. Its origins date back to the 13th century, and it played a significant role in Scotland's Wars of Independence. The castle was the site of numerous battles between the Scots and the English, particularly during the reign of Edward I of England. Though much of the castle was dismantled in the 17th century to prevent it from being used by Jacobite forces, its history remains closely tied to the region's tumultuous past.

LOCATION

Urquhart Castle is located on the shore of Loch Ness, near the village of Drumnadrochit, about 15 miles southwest of Inverness in the Scottish Highlands. Its position offers dramatic views of Loch Ness and the surrounding hills, making it one of the most scenic castles in Scotland.

ARCHITECTURAL FEATURES

Though in ruins today, Urquhart Castle features a classic design for a medieval Scottish fortress, including a central courtyard, a large keep, and defensive walls. The castle's most notable feature is the 16th-century Grant Tower, which offers panoramic views of Loch Ness. The castle's defensive walls and towers were once built to withstand siege and attacks, and remnants of the buildings and structures can still be explored by visitors.

INTERESTING FACTS

- Urquhart Castle was once one of the largest castles in Scotland, built and expanded from the 13th century onwards.
- The castle was largely destroyed in the 17th century, during the English Civil War, by government forces to prevent it from falling into the hands of Jacobites.
- The site is now one of the most visited in Scotland, offering spectacular views of Loch Ness and the surrounding landscape.

NOTEWORTHY SURROUNDINGS

The stunning setting of Urquhart Castle on Loch Ness makes it a must-see for visitors to the Highlands. The surrounding area is famous for its connections to the Loch Ness Monster, with nearby boat tours offering the opportunity to search the lake for the elusive creature. The castle's proximity to the village of Drumnadrochit offers visitors access to local shops, cafes, and the Loch Ness Centre and Exhibition.

EILEAN DONAN CASTLE
HIGHLANDS, SCOTLAND

HISTORICAL SIGNIFICANCE

Eilean Donan Castle is one of Scotland's most iconic castles, built on a small island at the point where three lochs meet—Loch Duich, Loch Long, and Loch Alsh. Originally constructed in the 13th century, it was strategically positioned to protect the region from Viking invasions. The castle was almost destroyed during the Jacobite uprising of 1719 but was painstakingly rebuilt in the early 20th century. It is now one of Scotland's most photographed landmarks and is a symbol of Scottish heritage and history.

LOCATION

Eilean Donan Castle is located in the Scottish Highlands, on a small tidal island at the point where the three lochs meet. It is approximately 1.5 miles from the village of Dornie, in the region of Highland Scotland, and is easily accessible by car via a bridge that connects the island to the mainland.

ARCHITECTURAL FEATURES

Eilean Donan Castle is a stunning example of Scottish baronial architecture, with thick stone walls, a large keep, and imposing towers. The castle's location on a small island and its dramatic setting make it a particularly picturesque structure. The 20th-century restoration preserved its medieval features while enhancing the structure to make it a grand and impressive sight. Inside, the castle contains period furnishings, artwork, and artifacts that reflect its long history.

INTERESTING FACTS

- Eilean Donan Castle was built in the 13th century by Alexander II to protect the region from Viking invasions.
- The castle was destroyed by government forces during the Jacobite uprising of 1719 but was rebuilt in the early 20th century by the MacRae family.
- It became famous worldwide when it appeared in films such as The Highlander and James Bond: The World Is Not Enough.

NOTEWORTHY SURROUNDINGS

The castle's picturesque location, surrounded by lochs and mountains, makes it one of the most beautiful castles in Scotland. The surrounding area is ideal for walking, hiking, and sightseeing, with numerous trails that offer spectacular views of the castle and its stunning natural environment. The nearby Skye Bridge provides access to the Isle of Skye, a popular destination for nature lovers and hikers.

DUNNOTTAR CASTLE
ABERDEENSHIRE, SCOTLAND

Dunnottar Castle is a dramatic and historic fortress perched on a rocky cliff on the northeastern coast of Scotland. It has a rich history, with roots dating back to at least the 14th century. Dunnottar played a crucial role during the Wars of Scottish Independence, and it was here that the Scottish Crown Jewels were hidden to prevent them from falling into English hands during the 17th century. The castle was also involved in the Jacobite uprisings before falling into ruin.

LOCATION

Dunnottar Castle is located in Aberdeenshire, on the eastern coast of Scotland, approximately 2 miles south of Stonehaven. The castle sits atop a cliff, offering dramatic views over the North Sea. Its isolated location on the edge of the coast makes it a striking and memorable site to visit.

ARCHITECTURAL FEATURES

The castle is built on a rocky promontory and is accessed by a narrow causeway. Its defensive features include high walls, gates, and a series of towers, including a 15th-century keep. The site's natural geography, with steep cliffs on three sides, provided a formidable defense against attackers. Despite being largely in ruins today, Dunnottar Castle remains an impressive site, with the remains of the royal chambers, the chapel, and the outer walls still visible.

INTERESTING FACTS

- Dunnottar Castle played a crucial role in Scottish history, especially during the Wars of Scottish Independence and the 17th century when it held the Scottish Crown Jewels.
- The castle was almost destroyed in the 18th century but was saved by local efforts and remains a popular tourist attraction.
- The castle's isolated location on a cliff makes it one of Scotland's most photogenic and dramatic sites.

NOTEWORTHY SURROUNDINGS

The rugged coastline surrounding Dunnottar Castle is as breathtaking as the castle itself, with steep cliffs, crashing waves, and scenic walking trails. The nearby village of Stonehaven offers accommodations, restaurants, and charming local shops. Visitors can explore the coastal paths, which provide stunning views of the castle perched above the sea. The area is also known for its wildlife, including seabirds and marine life in the surrounding waters.

INVERARAY CASTLE
ARGYLL AND BUTE, SCOTLAND

HISTORICAL SIGNIFICANCE

Inveraray Castle is a beautiful Gothic-style castle located on the shores of Loch Fyne in western Scotland. It has been the seat of the Duke of Argyll and the chief of Clan Campbell since the 15th century. The castle played an important role in Scottish history, particularly during the Jacobite uprisings, when the Campbells were prominent supporters of the British Crown. The castle has been continually occupied by the Campbell family and remains their ancestral home.

LOCATION

Inveraray Castle is situated in the Argyll and Bute region of western Scotland, on the southern shore of Loch Fyne. It is located near the town of Inveraray, approximately 60 miles north of Glasgow.

ARCHITECTURAL FEATURES

Inveraray Castle is a striking example of Scottish Gothic Revival architecture, with its iconic turrets, pointed arches, and crenellated towers. The castle was designed by the famous architect Robert Mylne in the 18th century, though it incorporates elements from earlier medieval fortresses. The interiors are grand, with elaborate rooms, including a stunning library, dining hall, and several state rooms. The surrounding gardens and grounds are beautifully landscaped, with terraced gardens leading down to the loch.

INTERESTING FACTS

- Inveraray Castle has been the seat of the Duke of Argyll and Clan Campbell for over 500 years.
- The castle played an important role in the Jacobite uprisings, as the Campbells were staunch supporters of the British Crown.
- The castle's beautiful Gothic design and picturesque setting have made it a popular filming location for TV shows and movies, including Downton Abbey.

NOTEWORTHY SURROUNDINGS

Inveraray Castle is set in a stunning location on the shores of Loch Fyne, with sweeping views of the water and surrounding mountains. The town of Inveraray is known for its charming Georgian architecture, and it offers a range of shops, restaurants, and accommodation options. The surrounding area is perfect for hiking and exploring the natural beauty of Argyll, with nearby trails offering views of the loch and hills.

BALMORAL CASTLE
ABERDEENSHIRE, SCOTLAND

HISTORICAL SIGNIFICANCE

Balmoral Castle is a Scottish estate that has served as a royal residence for the British monarchy since it was purchased by Queen Victoria in 1852. The castle holds significant historical importance as it has been the summer home of the royal family, offering them a retreat from the pressures of public life. Queen Victoria and Prince Albert were instrumental in its construction and transformation into a royal retreat. The castle is still a private residence of the royal family today, with Queen Elizabeth II and other members of the royal family spending time there during their summer holidays.

LOCATION

Balmoral Castle is located in Aberdeenshire, in the heart of the Scottish Highlands. It is situated near the village of Crathie, just west of the River Dee. The picturesque location amidst the rolling hills and forests of the Highlands adds to the allure of the estate.

ARCHITECTURAL FEATURES

The castle was designed in a Scottish Baronial style, which combines elements of traditional Scottish and medieval architecture. The building is characterized by its high towers, turrets, and thick stone walls, with a prominent central keep. The estate's grounds feature extensive gardens, woodlands, and a large park, as well as a beautiful private chapel, which is regularly used by the royal family. The castle's interior is richly decorated, with elegant furnishings, royal portraits, and displays showcasing the family's history.

INTERESTING FACTS

- Balmoral Castle is still privately owned by the royal family, unlike other royal residences that belong to the Crown.
- The estate has been passed down through generations of the royal family, and it holds special personal significance to them, particularly Queen Victoria and Prince Albert, who greatly enjoyed their time there.
- Balmoral is famously known for its connection to the British royal family's love of outdoor pursuits like hunting, fishing, and hiking in the surrounding hills.

NOTEWORTHY SURROUNDINGS

The surrounding Scottish Highlands are known for their rugged beauty, with nearby mountains, forests, and the River Dee offering opportunities for hiking, fishing, and wildlife watching. The area is a popular destination for those seeking a tranquil retreat, and visitors to the estate can explore the gardens and grounds, though the castle itself is only open to the public during certain times of the year.

HOLYROOD PALACE
EDINBURGH, SCOTLAND

Holyrood Palace is the official residence of the British monarch in Scotland. Located at the end of Edinburgh's famous Royal Mile, the palace has served as the residence of Scottish kings and queens for centuries. The history of Holyrood Palace is closely intertwined with Scotland's royal family, and it has witnessed significant events, such as the marriage of Mary, Queen of Scots, to Lord Darnley, and the murder of her secretary, David Rizzio, in 1566. Today, it remains the monarch's official residence when they are in Scotland and is used for ceremonial and state functions.

LOCATION

Holyrood Palace is located at the end of Edinburgh's Royal Mile, at the foot of Arthur's Seat in Edinburgh, Scotland. It sits at the heart of the city, offering a majestic view of the surrounding area, including the extinct volcano of Arthur's Seat and the picturesque Holyrood Park.

ARCHITECTURAL FEATURES

The palace was originally founded in the 12th century and has undergone several architectural changes over the centuries. Today, it combines medieval, Renaissance, and Baroque elements. The central quadrangle, with its tall, elegant towers, is a striking feature, while the state apartments, including the royal chambers, are richly furnished with period pieces and royal artifacts. The ruins of the Abbey of Holyrood, which once stood on the site, are also a significant feature, offering insight into the palace's long and storied history.

INTERESTING FACTS

- Holyrood Palace has been the residence of Scottish kings and queens for centuries, including being the home of Mary, Queen of Scots.
- The palace is open to the public year-round, offering visitors a chance to explore the lavish royal apartments and gardens.
- It is also the site of many ceremonial events, including royal investitures and state occasions.

NOTEWORTHY SURROUNDINGS

Holyrood Park, which surrounds the palace, is a large public park that includes the famous Arthur's Seat, a dormant volcano offering panoramic views of the city. Visitors to Holyrood Palace can take a walk through the park, explore the ruins of Holyrood Abbey, or hike up to Arthur's Seat for a breathtaking view of Edinburgh and beyond.

MELROSE ABBEY
SCOTTISH BORDERS, SCOTLAND

While not technically a castle, Melrose Abbey is an important historical site that should not be overlooked by those interested in Scotland's royal and religious history. Founded in 1136 by King David I, it was a Cistercian monastery that played a significant role in the medieval Scottish church. It is particularly famous for being the burial site of Robert the Bruce's heart, which was brought back here after his death during the Crusades. The abbey's historical importance lies not just in its religious function but also in its association with Scottish royalty and its architectural grandeur.

LOCATION

Melrose Abbey is located in the town of Melrose in the Scottish Borders, around 35 miles south of Edinburgh. The site sits in a beautiful valley on the banks of the River Tweed, making it a picturesque and tranquil location.

ARCHITECTURAL FEATURES

Melrose Abbey is renowned for its stunning architecture, which blends Romanesque and Gothic styles. The remains of the abbey include the nave, transepts, and stunning decorative elements, such as the intricate stone carvings and the remnants of the abbey's medieval stained glass. The most iconic feature is the East Window, with its beautiful tracery and ornamental stonework. The abbey is also notable for its unusual and ornate burial place for Robert the Bruce's heart, a site marked by a commemorative plaque.

INTERESTING FACTS

- Melrose Abbey was founded by King David I of Scotland in 1136 as part of a Cistercian monastic foundation.
- It is the final resting place of Robert the Bruce's heart, which was carried by his commander Sir James Douglas on a crusade to Spain before being buried at Melrose.
- The abbey was partially destroyed during the Reformation and further damaged by English troops during the 1545 invasion but remains a stunning example of medieval architecture.

NOTEWORTHY SURROUNDINGS

The Scottish Borders region is known for its rolling hills, picturesque villages, and scenic landscapes, making Melrose Abbey a popular stop for visitors exploring the area. The town of Melrose offers charming shops, cafes, and local attractions, including the nearby Abbotsford House, the former home of author Sir Walter Scott. The tranquil River Tweed runs nearby, providing a lovely backdrop to the abbey's ruin.

DOUNE CASTLE
STIRLING, SCOTLAND

Doune Castle is a well-preserved medieval stronghold located near Stirling, Scotland. It dates back to the late 14th century and was originally built by Robert Stewart, Duke of Albany. Over the years, the castle served various functions, including being a royal residence and military stronghold. It played an important role in the Wars of Scottish Independence and was involved in several historical conflicts. While its historical significance is rooted in its use as a royal residence, it is perhaps most famous today for its role in popular culture.

LOCATION

Doune Castle is located about 8 miles northwest of Stirling, in central Scotland. It is situated on the River Teith, with views over the surrounding countryside and nearby hills.

ARCHITECTURAL FEATURES

Doune Castle is a classic example of a late 14th-century Scottish fortress, with a large rectangular plan, a central courtyard, and thick defensive walls. The castle features four corner towers, a large gatehouse, and a hall that once served as the royal residence. The design of the castle reflects both military needs and the comfort of its occupants, with a well-constructed great hall and other domestic rooms.

INTERESTING FACTS

- Doune Castle is famous for its appearances in the film Monty Python and the Holy Grail, where it served as the filming location for several scenes.
- The castle was also used as a filming location for the Outlander TV series, where it was portrayed as the fictional Castle Leoch.
- The castle is exceptionally well-preserved for its age and remains a popular destination for history enthusiasts and fans of the films and TV shows it featured in.

NOTEWORTHY SURROUNDINGS

The castle's setting in the beautiful Scottish countryside provides scenic views of the surrounding area, including the nearby hills and the River Teith. Visitors can explore the charming village of Doune, which offers quaint shops and local hospitality. The area is rich in history, with other nearby attractions such as Stirling Castle, the Wallace Monument, and the historic town of Stirling, all just a short drive away.

CRAIGNETHAN CASTLE
SOUTH LANARKSHIRE, SCOTLAND

HISTORICAL SIGNIFICANCE

Craignethan Castle, dating back to the mid-16th century, was built by the powerful Scottish noble family, the Cunninghams, and later passed into the hands of the Hamiltons. Its history is tied to the turbulent political climate of the time, with several notable events including its use as a defensive stronghold during conflicts such as the English invasions. It was also involved in the complex politics of the time, serving as a site of both defense and residence for the local nobility.

LOCATION

Craignethan Castle is located near the village of Crossford, South Lanarkshire, Scotland. It sits on a scenic plateau overlooking the River Nethan, providing both a strategic defensive position and a picturesque setting.

ARCHITECTURAL FEATURES

The castle is an excellent example of a mid-16th-century Scottish fortress, built primarily in the Renaissance style. It features a rectangular layout with a central courtyard and is surrounded by strong defensive walls, a tower house, and a gatehouse. The castle retains many original features, including a well-preserved spiral staircase and a variety of domestic chambers. The outer walls are still standing, offering visitors a glimpse of the structure's original design.

INTERESTING FACTS

- Craignethan Castle is often described as a "fortified mansion" due to its combination of defensive and residential features.
- The castle was abandoned in the 17th century, and although it is in a semi-ruined state, much of its charm lies in its well-preserved walls and battlements.
- The castle is lesser-known compared to other Scottish castles, making it a peaceful and quiet location for visitors.

NOTEWORTHY SURROUNDINGS

The castle is surrounded by the scenic Nethan Gorge and the rolling hills of South Lanarkshire, offering beautiful hiking opportunities. The nearby village of Crossford offers a quaint and picturesque atmosphere. The surrounding area is rich in natural beauty, making it a great spot for exploring the Scottish countryside.

CAERPHILLY CASTLE
CAERPHILLY, WALES

Caerphilly Castle, built in the 13th century by Gilbert de Clare, is one of the largest castles in Britain. It was constructed as part of the Norman conquest of Wales, designed to be a formidable fortress to control the region. The castle's impressive design and defensive features were created to ward off Welsh rebellions and solidify Norman control over the area. It played an important role in the conflicts between the English crown and the Welsh princes.

LOCATION

Caerphilly Castle is located in the town of Caerphilly, South Wales, about 7 miles north of Cardiff. It lies in the heart of the town, surrounded by a large artificial lake that enhances its dramatic appearance.

ARCHITECTURAL FEATURES

Caerphilly Castle is an iconic example of medieval military architecture, with massive defensive walls, a deep moat, and an intricate system of ditches and water features. Its most notable architectural feature is the massive leaning tower, which is the second-largest of its kind in Britain, after the Leaning Tower of Pisa. The castle's walls are incredibly thick, and the structure includes a complex of inner and outer bailey walls, a central keep, and extensive gatehouses, making it a masterclass in military design.

INTERESTING FACTS

- Caerphilly Castle is the second-largest castle in Britain by area, after Windsor Castle.
- The famous leaning tower of the castle is an architectural anomaly, with its tilt a result of unstable foundations and subsiding land.
- The castle has been extensively restored and is a popular tourist attraction, hosting events, reenactments, and festivals.

NOTEWORTHY SURROUNDINGS

The castle is set within its own artificial lake and is surrounded by extensive grounds. The picturesque town of Caerphilly is located nearby, offering a variety of shops, cafes, and local landmarks. The area is a great place to explore for those interested in Welsh history and heritage, with nearby attractions such as the town's 13th-century church and beautiful local parks.

CARDIFF CASTLE
CARDIFF, WALES

Cardiff Castle is a historic site with a rich history spanning Roman, Norman, and Victorian periods. Originally a Roman fort, it was transformed into a medieval Norman castle by the de Clare family in the 11th century. In the 19th century, the castle was extensively remodeled into a lavish Gothic-style mansion by the third Marquess of Bute. The castle has seen centuries of history, from Roman occupation to medieval conflicts and Victorian opulence.

LOCATION

Cardiff Castle is located in the heart of Cardiff, the capital of Wales. The castle grounds are situated near the city center, making it an easily accessible and central landmark for visitors.

ARCHITECTURAL FEATURES

The castle combines a variety of architectural styles, from its Roman and Norman roots to the extravagant Victorian Gothic renovations. The medieval keep and the Norman gatehouse are notable elements, as are the Roman walls that remain buried beneath the castle's foundations. The Victorian remodeling introduced lavish interiors, including ornate woodwork, elaborate murals, and stained glass windows, with the Castle's Clock Tower and the Bute Tower standing out as examples of Gothic Revival architecture.

INTERESTING FACTS

- Cardiff Castle was originally a Roman fort, and remnants of the Roman walls can still be seen today.
- The castle was transformed into a Victorian Gothic mansion by the third Marquess of Bute, one of the wealthiest men in Britain at the time.
- Cardiff Castle has been used for various purposes over the years, including as a military barracks during World War II.

NOTEWORTHY SURROUNDINGS

Cardiff Castle is centrally located within Cardiff's city center, meaning visitors can easily explore the surrounding area. The castle grounds are surrounded by beautiful parkland, including Bute Park, which is ideal for leisurely walks. Nearby, visitors can enjoy Cardiff's thriving cultural and shopping scene, with the Principality Stadium, National Museum Cardiff, and the bustling Cardiff Market all within walking distance.

HARLECH CASTLE
GWYNEDD, WALES

HISTORICAL SIGNIFICANCE

Harlech Castle, built in the late 13th century by Edward I during his conquest of Wales, is a UNESCO World Heritage site. The castle played a pivotal role in the struggles between the English crown and the Welsh during the Wars of Welsh Independence. Harlech Castle famously withstood a lengthy siege during the Welsh rebellion led by the last Welsh prince, Llywelyn ap Gruffudd. The castle's strategic location and robust defensive design made it an important military stronghold in Wales.

LOCATION

Harlech Castle is located in the town of Harlech in Gwynedd, North Wales. It sits dramatically atop a rocky outcrop with views over the surrounding landscape, including the Irish Sea and Snowdonia. The castle's location was chosen for its natural defensive advantages, offering commanding views of the surrounding area.

ARCHITECTURAL FEATURES

Harlech Castle is an excellent example of Edward I's concentric castle design, with multiple layers of walls, gates, and towers to create a nearly impenetrable fortress. The most impressive feature is the castle's massive walls, built using local stone, and the large central courtyard. The design of the castle allows for defense from every direction, with its watchtowers offering panoramic views of the surrounding terrain.

INTERESTING FACTS

- Harlech Castle was one of the "iron ring" castles built by Edward I to solidify English control over Wales.
- The castle was besieged multiple times during the Welsh uprisings and during the English Civil War.
- The castle was featured in the popular Welsh song "Men of Harlech," which commemorates the castle's legendary siege.

NOTEWORTHY SURROUNDINGS

The castle offers stunning views of the surrounding countryside, including the dunes of Harlech Beach and the Snowdonia mountain range. Visitors can enjoy a scenic walk along the nearby coastline, with the North Wales coast providing opportunities for hiking and exploring. The town of Harlech itself is charming, with quaint shops and local attractions, including the nearby Royal St. David's Golf Club.

BEAUMARIS CASTLE
ANGLESEY, WALES

HISTORICAL SIGNIFICANCE

Beaumaris Castle, located on the island of Anglesey, is a UNESCO World Heritage site renowned for its architectural brilliance. Built between 1295 and 1330 under the orders of Edward I during his conquest of Wales, Beaumaris was designed as a part of the "Iron Ring" of castles that Edward I constructed to subdue Welsh resistance. Although it was never fully completed, the castle remains a masterpiece of military architecture, featuring some of the most advanced design elements of its time, including concentric walls and a sophisticated defensive system.

LOCATION

Beaumaris Castle is located in the town of Beaumaris on the Isle of Anglesey, North Wales, overlooking the Menai Strait and providing views towards the Snowdonia mountain range. Its location was chosen to control access to the strait and as part of Edward I's military strategy to secure the region.

ARCHITECTURAL FEATURES

Beaumaris Castle is one of the finest examples of concentric castle design, featuring multiple layers of defensive walls. The castle has a circular plan, with an inner and outer bailey, multiple defensive walls, a deep moat, and a strong gatehouse. The design was intended to make the castle almost impregnable, with a labyrinth of defensive features such as a water-filled moat, drawbridges, and multiple entrances. The castle's impressive towers and a great hall were meant to serve both defensive and residential purposes.

INTERESTING FACTS

- Beaumaris Castle is considered the pinnacle of medieval military architecture but was never fully completed due to budget and time constraints.
- It is one of the last castles built by Edward I as part of his conquest of Wales.
- Despite its unfinished status, the castle remains remarkably intact and is a popular tourist destination.

NOTEWORTHY SURROUNDINGS

The castle is located near Beaumaris town, with views over the Menai Strait towards the mainland of Wales. The town itself is picturesque, with charming Georgian architecture and a historic pier. Beaumaris offers access to the beautiful Anglesey coastline, which is perfect for scenic walks and exploring local beaches. Nearby attractions include the Beaumaris Gaol and the town's well-preserved Victorian architecture.

LLANGOLLEN CASTLE
DENBIGHSHIRE, WALES

Llangollen Castle, located in the village of Llangollen, Denbighshire, was built in the early 13th century. It is a relatively small castle, constructed during the reign of King Edward I as part of the military infrastructure for controlling the Welsh Marches. Over time, Llangollen Castle has undergone various transformations, and while it was once a fortress, it later became a private residence. Today, the castle is more of a ruin, but it still holds historical importance as a defensive structure in a turbulent region.

LOCATION

Llangollen Castle is situated on the southern banks of the River Dee, in the picturesque town of Llangollen, North Wales. The site is surrounded by lush landscapes, including hills and the nearby Berwyn Mountains, giving it dramatic and scenic views of the Welsh countryside.

ARCHITECTURAL FEATURES

Llangollen Castle features a simple yet effective design typical of smaller castles built during the medieval period. The remaining structure includes a large stone tower and parts of the curtain walls. The castle was originally designed to defend the area from external threats, and its location provided a strategic position over the River Dee. Although much of the castle has been lost over time, its imposing position on a hill still offers a commanding view of the surrounding area.

INTERESTING FACTS

- Llangollen Castle was associated with the Welsh lordship of Bromfield and Yale, and it is believed that it served as a home for the local nobility.
- The castle is not as well-known as some of the larger Welsh fortresses, making it a quiet and peaceful destination for visitors.
- The castle has strong ties to the surrounding countryside, with its positioning in the scenic Dee Valley adding to its charm.

NOTEWORTHY SURROUNDINGS

Llangollen Castle is set amidst the natural beauty of the Dee Valley, and visitors can enjoy scenic walks through the surrounding hills and woodlands. The town of Llangollen itself is famous for its historic steam railway, the Llangollen Railway, and its proximity to the Pontcysyllte Aqueduct, a UNESCO World Heritage site. The area is also known for the Llangollen International Musical Eisteddfod, a celebration of music and culture.

CRICCIETH CASTLE
GWYNEDD, WALES

Criccieth Castle, located on the North Wales coast, was built by Llywelyn the Great in the 13th century before being taken over by Edward I as part of his conquest of Wales. The castle played an important role in defending Gwynedd and the Welsh coastline from the English. It also witnessed several sieges during the Welsh uprisings, making it a symbol of both Welsh independence and the struggle against English domination.

LOCATION

Criccieth Castle is situated on a promontory overlooking Cardigan Bay in Gwynedd, North Wales. The location offers stunning views of the bay, the nearby mountains, and the surrounding coastline, making it a visually striking site.

ARCHITECTURAL FEATURES

The castle is a classic example of a Welsh coastal fortress, built on a headland to take advantage of natural defensive features. The castle's design includes a small inner courtyard, defensive walls, and a large round tower. The outer walls are rugged and less symmetrical than some other castles, adding to its charm. The circular keep, which is one of the most recognizable features of Criccieth Castle, still stands as a prominent reminder of its past.

INTERESTING FACTS

- Criccieth Castle was one of the last castles to be taken by the English in their conquest of Wales.
- The castle has two distinct architectural styles, reflecting its origins as a Welsh fortress before being captured by the English.
- The castle has been partially restored, and today it remains an important tourist attraction.

NOTEWORTHY SURROUNDINGS

The castle offers panoramic views over Cardigan Bay, with vistas stretching across the coastline and the mountains of Snowdonia in the distance. Criccieth itself is a charming seaside town, known for its beautiful beaches and traditional Welsh hospitality. The area is ideal for hiking, with several scenic trails that offer spectacular views of the surrounding landscapes. Nearby attractions include the picturesque village of Portmeirion and Snowdonia National Park.

CARRICKFERGUS CASTLE
COUNTY ANTRIM, NORTHERN IRELAND

Carrickfergus Castle is one of the best-preserved medieval castles in Northern Ireland and has played a key role in the history of the region. Built in 1177 by John de Courcy, an Anglo-Norman knight, it served as a strategic military stronghold throughout the Middle Ages. The castle was central to English control over Ireland and saw numerous battles, sieges, and attacks. Notably, it withstood a siege by the Scots in 1315 and later played an important role in the English Civil War. It also served as a military garrison for several centuries.

LOCATION

Carrickfergus Castle is located in the town of Carrickfergus, County Antrim, Northern Ireland, along the shores of Belfast Lough. Its position by the water was strategically chosen to guard the entrance to the lough and to control maritime traffic coming into Belfast.

ARCHITECTURAL FEATURES

Carrickfergus Castle is a classic example of Norman military architecture, built from local basalt rock. The castle features a rectangular layout with a large keep and defensive walls, a dry moat, and a gatehouse with a drawbridge. The keep, with its high stone walls, offers excellent views over the surrounding coastline and town. The castle's strong defensive features, including its fortified walls and towers, reflect its purpose as a fortress meant to withstand prolonged sieges.

INTERESTING FACTS

- Carrickfergus Castle is one of the best-preserved examples of a Norman castle in Ireland, with much of its structure remaining intact.
- The castle was the site of the landing of King William III of England in 1690 before the Battle of the Boyne.
- It served as a military garrison until the early 20th century and has been used for various military purposes throughout its history.

NOTEWORTHY SURROUNDINGS

Carrickfergus Castle is situated on the edge of Carrickfergus, which is a historic town with a vibrant maritime heritage. The town offers scenic views of Belfast Lough and is a gateway for exploring nearby natural attractions, such as the Antrim Coast. Nearby, you can also visit the Carrickfergus Museum, which provides further insight into the history of the castle and the surrounding region.

BUCKINGHAM PALACE
LONDON, ENGLAND

Buckingham Palace is one of the most famous royal residences in the world and serves as the official London residence of the British monarch. It has been the administrative headquarters of the monarchy since Queen Victoria's accession in 1837. While originally built as a private house in the early 18th century, it was transformed into a royal palace in the 19th century. Over the years, it has been a central location for state occasions, royal ceremonies, and events that are significant to the British public, including coronations, jubilees, and royal weddings.

LOCATION

Buckingham Palace is located in the heart of London, surrounded by St. James's Park, Green Park, and the bustling streets of Westminster. Its central location makes it a key attraction in the city and an iconic symbol of the British monarchy.

ARCHITECTURAL FEATURES

The palace's neoclassical facade is one of its most recognized features, designed by architect John Nash and later altered by Edward Blore. The palace has 775 rooms, including 19 state rooms, 52 royal and guest bedrooms, 188 staff bedrooms, 92 offices, and 78 bathrooms. Its opulent interior is adorned with chandeliers, fine art, and elaborate furnishings. The balcony overlooking the Mall is one of its most famous architectural elements, often used for public appearances by the royal family during significant events.

INTERESTING FACTS

- Buckingham Palace was originally known as "Buckingham House" and was built for the Duke of Buckingham in 1703.
- The palace survived multiple bombings during World War II, with King George VI and Queen Elizabeth (the Queen Mother) famously staying in London during the Blitz to boost morale.
- The Changing of the Guard ceremony, held outside the palace, is one of the most popular traditions for visitors to witness.

NOTEWORTHY SURROUNDINGS

Buckingham Palace is surrounded by several landmarks and green spaces. St. James's Park, Green Park, and Hyde Park are nearby, offering tranquil retreats in the bustling city. The Mall, a grand avenue leading to Trafalgar Square, is lined with trees and Union flags, providing a stately approach to the palace. Westminster Abbey, the Houses of Parliament, and Big Ben are also within walking distance.

HIGHCLERE CASTLE
HAMPSHIRE, ENGLAND

HISTORICAL SIGNIFICANCE

Highclere Castle is one of the most iconic and well-known stately homes in England, largely due to its role as the filming location for the popular television series Downton Abbey. However, its history dates back to the 17th century when the site was originally developed as a country house. The castle has been the seat of the Earls of Carnarvon for over 300 years, and it was transformed into its present form in the 19th century by the 3rd Earl of Carnarvon, who also funded the discovery of King Tutankhamun's tomb in Egypt.

LOCATION

Highclere Castle is situated in the county of Hampshire, England, within the stunning countryside of the South of England. The estate is located near the town of Newbury and is surrounded by over 1,000 acres of parkland and gardens.

ARCHITECTURAL FEATURES

Highclere Castle is an impressive example of Jacobethan architecture, a blend of Jacobean and Elizabethan styles, with features inspired by both Renaissance and Gothic elements. The castle has a striking facade with a large central tower, ornate windows, and elaborate stonework. Inside, the rooms are lavishly decorated with fine art, antique furniture, and rich tapestries. The grounds feature meticulously designed gardens, including a well-known herb garden and sweeping lawns.

INTERESTING FACTS

- Highclere Castle became internationally famous as the setting for Downton Abbey, where it stood in for the fictional "Downton Abbey" estate.
- The 5th Earl of Carnarvon, who lived at Highclere, was famously involved in the discovery of King Tutankhamun's tomb in Egypt in 1922.
- The castle contains a vast collection of Egyptian artifacts, many related to the discovery of King Tut's tomb.

NOTEWORTHY SURROUNDINGS

Highclere Castle is set in beautiful Hampshire countryside, with sprawling gardens, parkland, and woodlands offering a serene atmosphere. The nearby village of Highclere and the town of Newbury provide additional charm with their historic buildings and quaint shops. The estate is also close to the North Wessex Downs Area of Outstanding Natural Beauty, which offers excellent walking and hiking opportunities.

BRITISH CASTLES

As we close the pages of this journey through Britain's most captivating castles, we at Bondi Publishing want to extend our heartfelt thanks to you, our reader, for embarking on this adventure with us. From the towering battlements of Windsor Castle to the windswept ruins of Tintagel, we hope this book has inspired a deeper appreciation for the history, architecture, and stories that have shaped these timeless landmarks.

Each castle tells its own tale of ambition, resilience, and legacy, and it is through your curiosity and passion that these stories continue to live on. Whether you've discovered new destinations to visit or simply enjoyed wandering through the pages, we hope this book has sparked your imagination and ignited a desire to explore the rich tapestry of Britain's heritage.

Thank you for joining us on this remarkable voyage. May your own adventures, whether through history or life itself, be as majestic and inspiring as the castles we've celebrated together.

Until next time,

The Bondi Publishing Team

Made in the USA
Monee, IL
02 August 2025

22455121R00059